James Bowie

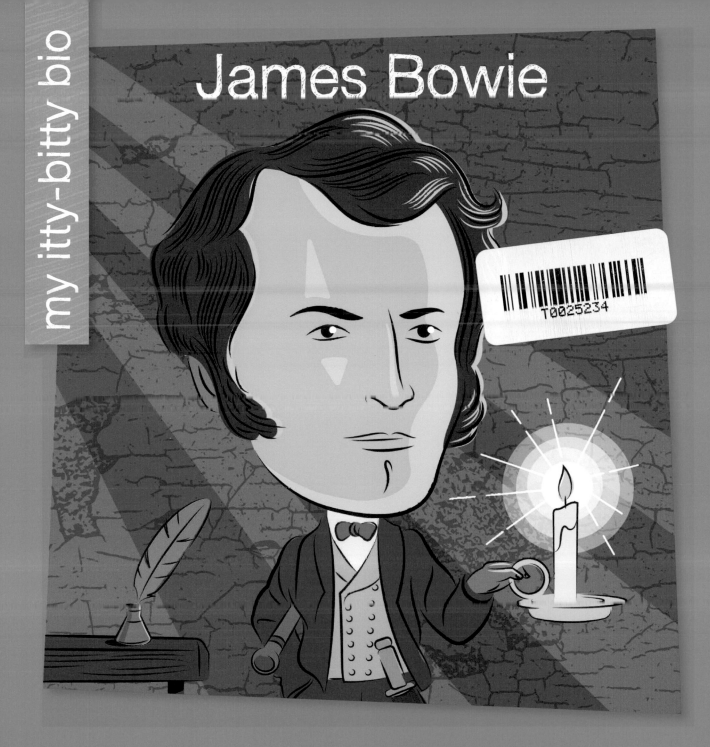

Published in the United States of America by Cherry Lake Publishing
Ann Arbor, Michigan
www.cherrylakepublishing.com

Reading Adviser: Marla Conn, MS, Ed, Literacy specialist, Read-Ability, Inc.
Book Designer: Jennifer Wahi
Illustrator: Jeff Bane

Photo Credits: ©Morphart Creation/Shutterstock, 5; ©Oleg Golovnev/Shutterstock, 7; ©Everett Collection/
Shutterstock, 9; ©Alfred Rudolph, artist/Library of Congress/Reproduction No. LC-USZ62-107717, 11, 22; ©robert
cicchetti/Shutterstock, 13, 23; ©Nic Tengg (Firm)/University of Houston Digital Library/File name: fpc238.jpg, 15;
©The Miriam and Ira D. Wallach Division of Art, Prints and Photographs: Print Collection/The New York Public
Library Digital Collections/UUID: 6a0138c0-db53-0130-fe7b-58d385a7b928, 17; ©Avaniks/Shutterstock, 19;
©Library of Congress/Reproduction No. LC-DIG-highsm-26035, 21; Jeff Bane, cover, 1, 6, 12, 16

Library of Congress Cataloging-in-Publication Data

Names: Sarantou, Katlin, author. | Bane, Jeff, 1957- illustrator.
Title: James Bowie / by Katlin Sarantou ; illustrated by Jeff Bane.
Description: Ann Arbor, MI : Cherry Lake Publishing, [2019] | Series: My
    itty-bitty bio | Includes bibliographical references and index. |
    Audience: Grades K-3.
Identifiers: LCCN 2019004210| ISBN 9781534147058 (hardcover) | ISBN
    9781534148482 (pdf) | ISBN 9781534149915 (pbk.) | ISBN 9781534151345
    (hosted ebook)
Subjects: LCSH: Bowie, Jim, 1796?-1836--Juvenile literature. |
    Pioneers--Texas--Biography--Juvenile literature. | Alamo (San Antonio,
    Tex.)--Siege, 1836--Juvenile literature. | Texas--History--To
    1846--Juvenile literature. | Frontier and pioneer life--Texas--Juvenile
    literature.
Classification: LCC F389.B8 S27 2019 | DDC 976.4/03092 [B] --dc23
LC record available at https://lccn.loc.gov/2019004210

Printed in the United States of America
Corporate Graphics

table of contents

About the author: Katlin Sarantou grew up in the cornfields of Ohio. She enjoys reading and dreaming of faraway places.

About the illustrator: Jeff Bane and his two business partners own a studio along the American River in Folsom, California, home of the 1849 Gold Rush. When Jeff's not sketching or illustrating for clients, he's either swimming or kayaking in the river to relax.

I was born in 1796 in Kentucky.

I grew up in Louisiana.

I grew up on the farm. I planted **crops.**

I learned how to fish. I learned how to hunt.

What else do you do on a farm?

I also learned how to read and write. I could speak Spanish and French.

What languages can you speak?

My brothers and I bought a **plantation**.

We set up a **steam mill**. It was the first in Louisiana.

I heard stories about Texas.
It was a land of **opportunity**.

I moved there to start fresh.
I did this in 1828.

Is there somewhere you'd like to live?

I joined the Texas army. I was in many battles. I was a **colonel**.

I was an important figure in the Texas Revolution.

I was a skilled fighter. There is a knife named after me.

FORT BROWN, TEXAS.—[FROM A SKETCH BY A GOVERNMENT PHOTOGRAPHER.—[SEE PAGE 211.]

FORT LANCASTER, TEXAS.—[FROM A SKETCH BY A GOVERNMENT PHOTOGRAPHER.—[SEE PAGE 211.]

My most famous battle was the Battle of the Alamo.

I died in this battle.

You may have heard stories about me.

Some are true. Others are not.

I have become a **folk hero** and a **legend**.

What would you like to ask me?

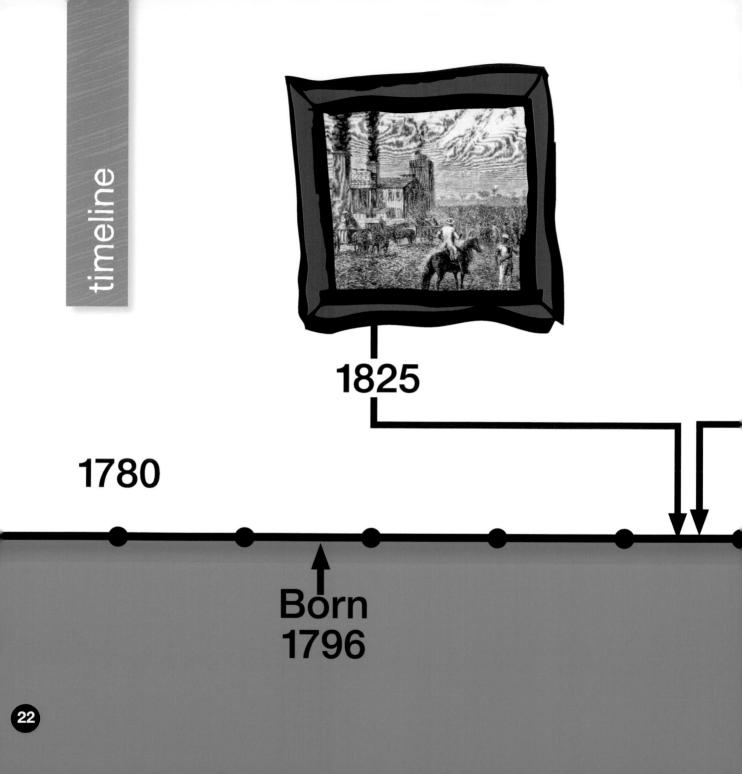

1825

1780

Born
1796

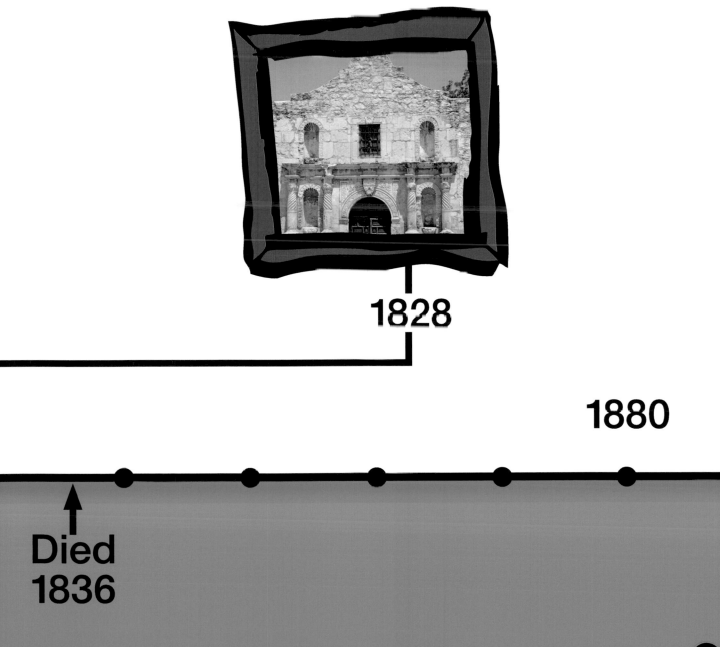

1828

1880

Died
1836

glossary

colonel (KUR-nuhl) a rank of an officer in the army

crops (KRAHPS) plants

folk hero (FOHK HEER-oh) a person who is greatly liked and respected by people in an area

legend (LEJ-uhnd) someone who is famous or well known for something

opportunity (ah-pur-TOO-nih-tee) a chance or a good time to do something

plantation (plan-TAY-shuhn) a large farm often worked by slaves

steam mill (STEEM MIL) a mill powered by steam that grinds things into small pieces

index